Lazy Programmers
The Good, the Bad and the Ugly

By Michael C. Daconta

Table of Contents

List of Figures

List of Source Code

Acknowledgements

This is the first technical book I have written in a while, and it feels really good to be back in this space. Sort of like slipping into your favorite pair of jeans or sliding behind the wheel of a comfortable ride – it just feels "right".

I would like to thank my family, friends and colleagues that support me in all my endeavours. First is family – we are a close-knit bunch and getting closer every day. There is no filter and lots of laughter. I am so blessed to have you all in my life! To my sweetheart, Lynne, who stands by my side, holds me when times are tough and loves me for who I am: thank you. To my nephew Jeremy Belden, thank you for helping us every day without fail, without complaint and with joy in your heart. You are a true blessing to us! Special thanks to my brother, Joseph Daconta, for helping me with the cover layout.

To my friends and colleagues – it is so much fun to laugh, play and plan things together. You add a richness, levity and vitality to my life that refreshes me. Special thanks to my early reviewers – Shawn Vettom, Dave Boyd, Ed Danis, Tony Hong, Scott Hellenbach, Raymond Chian, Kevin T. Smith and Dan Green. Very special thanks to Bo Hong for creating an amazing cover illustration! She is a truly gifted graphics artist who is destined for great things!

To my fans and readers, let's keep exploring this wonderful world together!

Warm wishes,

Michael C. Daconta
Woodbridge, VA

Chapter 1 Introduction

In my 32 years of software development, I have worked my way up through every programming position from software engineer (level 1, 2, 3), Systems Analyst, Systems Architect (level 1, 2, 3), Team Leader, Chief Developer, Technical Director, Chief Scientist, Director, Chief Technology Officer and eventually various Vice President positions. That list of positions is not to impress you; instead, it is to illustrate the breadth of my experience to include working with every type of programmer: young and old, stupid and smart, cautious and bold, and even lazy (lazy-good, lazy-bad and lazy-ugly[1] as we shall see). I have seen this issue from both sides by being the manager of a self-described "lazy programmer" and from tackling technical debt caused by the layman's definition of laziness (the reluctance or disinclination to work). Given the tension caused by this ambiguity, I decided it is high time to settle this controversy.

Why is "Lazy Programming" controversial?

Lazy programming is controversial because there are many articles on the web that praise laziness as a virtue[2]. That this flies in the face of the common definition of laziness is obvious. Here is the definition of lazy from Wiktionary[3]:

Lazy (adjective) –

---

[1] "The Good, The Bad and the Ugly" is also a movie starring Clint Eastwood and created by United Artists. The phrase is used here in accordance with "fair use".
[2] Lenssen, Philip; "Why Good Programmers Are Lazy and Dumb"; http://blogoscoped.com/archive/2005-08-24-n14.html
[3] https://en.wiktionary.org/wiki/lazy

1. Unwilling to do work or make an effort; disinclined to exertion.

2. Causing or characterized by idleness; relaxed or leisurely.

3. Showing a lack of effort or care.

4. Sluggish; slow-moving.

5. Lax.

6. (of a cattle brand) Turned so that (the letter) is horizontal instead of vertical.

7. (computing theory) Employing lazy evaluation; not calculating results until they are immediately required.

8. (Britain, obsolete or dialect) Wicked; vicious.

Some programmers even take this one step further and praise laziness as even a characteristic of "great" programmers. For proof of this, they point to quotes from well known programmers like Bill Gates and Larry Wall. Bill Gates is often attributed[4] the quote, "I choose a lazy person to do a hard job. Because a lazy person will find an easy way to do it." While that may be wrongly attributed to Bill Gates, Larry Wall wrote in the book, "Programming Perl", about the three virtues of a programmer. The glossary contains this definition of Laziness:

"The quality that makes you go to great effort to reduce overall energy expenditure. It makes you write labor-saving programs that other people will find useful, and document what you wrote so you don't have to answer so many questions about it. Hence, the first great virtue of a programmer. Also hence, this book. See also impatience and hubris."[5]

---

[4] https://www.goodreads.com/quotes/568877-i-choose-a-lazy-person-to-do-a-hard-job NOTE: Quote Investigator found no evidence for this, see: https://quoteinvestigator.com/2014/02/26/lazy-job/

[5] Wall, Larry et. Al; Programming Perl; O'Reilly & Associates, Inc.; © 1996; Pg 609.

We will dig into detail on Larry Wall's definition of laziness in the next chapter, for now we only want to focus on the attribution of a negative characteristic to a person as a mark of greatness. Is this word play or language trick useful for the development of software engineering as a professional discipline? And this now brings us to the purpose of this book – to answer simple questions like this:

"For skill development and the furtherance of your career, is Laziness a Virtue or Vice?"

"For a team leader, should you develop Laziness in your junior developers or squash it like a bad habit?"

"For the profession of programming as an engineering discipline, does Laziness enhance or reduce the respect our profession garners from society at large?"

This book will strive to answer these questions for you by examining the practices, hype and reality of "lazy programming".

To cover this topic from multiple angles, the perspective will sometimes switch between the roles of software developer, team leader and program manager. The context and required technical depth dictate which role is most appropriate. For software developers, code examples are provided (the website will contain examples in other languages). For team leaders, commentary and summary analysis is often provided to understand the ramification of the techniques on team dynamics. For program managers, system-level and program-level ramifications are highlighted. Let's begin this discussion with the "good news".

Chapter 2 The Good

The Ayn Rand book "The Virtue of Selfishness"[6] has a title that intentionally juxtaposes a negative concept with a positive one for the shock value it implies. And it works: right off the bat, the reader is interested to see how the author can pull off this miraculous combination of polar opposites. In the same manner, many programmers feel you can safely replace the word selfishness with laziness, giving us the "Virtue of Laziness". Should that have been the title of this book? We will see in the end; however, it is safe to assume the title of this chapter is indeed, "The Virtue(s) of Laziness" as we will discuss the positive aspects of a "labor-saving" mindset. Let's walk through the most common ways that "Lazy programming" can be considered "good":

1. Lazy can mean "efficient".

Specifically, efficient in the long run. If a programmer performs a task repeatedly, then that programmer can save time "in the long run" by automating that task. If your version of "laziness" is to exploit every opportunity for automation then that is a good thing. Whether that should be called laziness or innovative is debatable; however, for now we can put that debate aside and focus on how this is accomplished. An obvious example of this is when you find yourself repeating the same terminal commands over and over. Programmer's save time by not repeating themselves in two ways: one via a simple command line shortcut called

---

[6] Rand, Ayn; The Virtue of Selfishness; © 1964; New American Library.

"aliasing". Many shell languages like Bash allow you to create a short alias for longer commands like this:

```
$ alias rm='rm -i'
$ alias ll = 'ls -al --color'
$ alias untar='tar -zxvf '
```

As you can see, an alias is an abbreviation for a longer command that saves the developer typing. You may be thinking, "Do we really count saving a few characters in a command as 'labor-saving'?" The answer is twofold: first, common commands will be used thousands and tens of thousands of times so all those saved keystrokes add up. Secondly, some aliases can be for longer commands and even multiple commands where the output of one is piped into the input of another like this:

```
$ alias psmem10='ps auxf | sort -nr -k 4 | head -10'
```

The above command would give you a list of the top 10 processes consuming memory on a linux system. The first command is *ps* which provides information on processes (running programs) and that output is piped into the *sort* command which is sorted based on the 4th column of output and that output is then piped to the *head* command which outputs the first n lines of input (in this case 10).

Now, let's move on to a better form of automation than mere abbreviations – automating repetitive tasks with a shell script.

Like most software developers, most of my day is consumed with our development cycle as depicted in Figure 1.

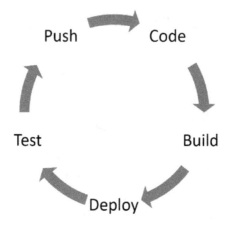

Figure 1 A Development Cycle

We do this over and over (sometimes not 'pushing' up the results to the feature branch until we have coded, tested and fixed the code multiple times). Regardless, of the exact sequence of steps, we do these things over and over so we again have an opportunity to save some labor by automating repetitive tasks.

I have scripts and aliases that help me through each of these phases. One of the most time consuming phases is patching the test instances to test a new change. Simply stated patching involves packaging up all my java archive files (jars) into a tar file, secure copying it over to a virtual machine based test server and unpacking it there. The pseudocode for the script is as follows:

```
cd /<parent-dir>
tar -cvzf mytar.tar.gz <src-dir>
scp mytar.tar.gz <remote-machine>:/<path>
cd /<deploy-dir>
tar -xvf mytar.tar.gz
rm mytar.tar.gz
```

Of course, the above commands are condensed and simplified from the actual script but you get the idea how a script file (a set of commands grouped into a single executable file), can save you a significant amount of time.

So, efficiencies can be achieved in the long-run by a bit of extra effort up front. This sort of "strategic laziness" (lose the battle but win the war) is a good thing. Another variant on this labor-saving theme is to find an easy way to do something hard.

2. Lazy can mean "creative".

The popular quote, "I choose a lazy person to do a hard job. Because a lazy person will find an easy way to do it", imbues the lazy person with a level of craftiness and creativity to find a "better way" than those industrious little ants that just "follow orders". While we could take this to mean the occasional flash of inspiration that saves millions of dollars in wasteful effort on the production line; instead, let's look at more common ways that programmer's find easier ways to do hard things. In my daily software development, I routinely use these techniques to make things easier: stack overflow, open source, and devops. Let's delve into each of these.

The website "stackoverflow"[7] is a Q&A site for programmers. It is often the number one search result returned by search engines for programming queries. At the time of this writing it's front page claims it has answers to 16.5 million questions. Questions are answered by a community of volunteers (similar to other crowd sourced sites like Wikipedia) that share their knowledge. Of course, a broader technique for this type of search is "googling" or using search engines to find an answer to a question. It is a good first

---

[7] https://stackoverflow.com

instinct to turn to your favorite search engine if you encounter an unknown problem in your work. In fact, many times if you receive an error message from any part of your system, you can cut and paste the exact error message into your browser and often see numerous responses from others who encountered the exact same error! Beyond using the search engine to answer problems of a small scope, another "lazy programmer" technique is required to tackle big problems like designing a new system, a new architecture, or major portions of a large system. This technique can be euphemistically called "OPC" or "Other People's Code"[8]. On the big data project that I support, we use hundreds (if not thousands) of open-source libraries and frameworks. Reuse of open-source software is a valuable technique to effectively speed up development of major systems. We use the React framework for our user interfaces, the Hadoop framework for parallel processing and many smaller libraries for custom visualization, caching, plotting, JSON processing, and much, much more.

Finally, on the creative front, modern IDEs and devops techniques (like virtual machines, puppet configuration and docker containers) are yet more evidence of labor-saving tools and innovations that have made the practice of programming more efficient.

3. Lazy coding techniques are part of the programmer's everyday vernacular.

Several common techniques have the word "lazy" in the expression, to include, "Lazy Instantiation", "Lazy Initialization" and "Lazy Evaluation". All of these techniques are related because lazy instantiation is a form of lazy initialization which is a form of lazy evaluation. Lazy

---

[8] This is a play off the common phrase "Other People's Money".

instantiation is delaying the creation of an object until it is needed. An example of this is when filling an Array as depicted in Listing 1.

Listing 1. LazyInstantiation

```
package us.daconta.lazy.programmers.examples;
import java.awt.image.BufferedImage;

public class LazyInstantiation {
    private static final int MAX_IMAGES=1000;
    private BufferedImage imageArray[];

    public BufferedImage getImage(int index) {
        if (imageArray == null) {
            // lazy instantiation
            imageArray = new BufferedImage[MAX_IMAGES];
        }

        if (index >= 0 && index < MAX_IMAGES) {
            if (imageArray[index] == null) {
                // lazy initialize the image here...
            }
            return imageArray[index];
        } else {
            return null;
        }
    }

    public static void main(String args[]) {
        LazyInstantiation lazy = new LazyInstantiation();
        BufferedImage myImage = lazy.getImage(100);
    }
}
```

In Listing 1 we see an example, where instead of creating the array of images as soon as the class is created (with the call of the no-arg constructor in the *main* method), we defer the creation of the imageArray until a user requests an image via the *getImage* method. Of course, the use of the term "Lazy" for these techniques is debatable. Should these really be called "lazy" when the term "deferred" works just as well? Of course not, however; many programmers delight in being snarky, clever and even counter-culture. It is a worn-out trope of Hollywood's incarnation of a hacker to be so smart that you don't need to follow any rules or any social norms for dress or behavior. Like Humpty Dumpty in the book <u>Alice in Wonderland</u>, programmers will sometimes use a word, term or expression sarcastically or obtusely in order to keep management off balance. Implying that "Lazy is Good" is part and parcel of a "you don't understand us" or "technical priesthood" mindset. As you can surmise, I believe the profession has no need for such childish cruft on its image or in its practice.

Similar to these explicitly "lazy" techniques, there are many similar efficiency techniques that are commonly used. Two popular ones are the D.R.Y. principle and caching. The "DRY principle" stands for the labor saving mantra, "Don't Repeat Yourself" and was coined by Andy Hunt and Dave Thomas in their book, <u>The Pragmatic Programmer</u>. The principle is stated like this: "Every piece of knowledge must have a single, unambiguous, authoritative representation within the system." A simple way in which I have seen this principle violated over the years (and admittedly, have even violated myself) is to "cut-and-paste" code from one class into another, sometimes in multiple places in the code. This is the worst form of replication because it ignores the danger of pasting something into a new context for the sake of minor expediency. So, here we have an interesting contrast: an example of what you would consider a good lazy habit (DRY) alongside an example of a "bad" lazy habit (cut-and-paste). The funny thing is that both could be and have been labeled as "lazy habits" just that one has the positive connotation of lazy and one has the negative connotation of lazy.

In the same vein as "lazy initialization" is the technique

of caching unchanged data. Caching is an efficiency technique of saving a potentially expensive, and more importantly unnecessary, data fetch operation. To do this, after data is fetched the first time it is stored in a memory cache. Then, upon a subsequent request, the data is retrieved from memory and not refreshed across the network (thus saving the expensive network operations of re-fetching the data from an external computer). We see this every day in modern web browsers that cache web pages after retrieving them.

These examples of "good" lazy techniques are the primary cause of this debate. They provide the fuel for the "pro-lazy" crowd to argue that "laziness is good" (which flies in the face of common sense). So, now let's begin to look at the other side of the equation.

Chapter 3 The Bad

I have personally managed a proud "lazy programmer" for seven years. During that time, I have seen the gamut of lazy behavior – yes, the good, the bad and the ugly. Let us now turn our attention to the dark side of laziness. That which actually conforms to its formal definition. There are three categories of "bad laziness" to watch out for: Shortcuts and Band-Aids; Sweeping dirt under the rug; and Avoiding architecture. Let's examine each of those categories in detail:

1. **Shortcuts and Band-Aids**.

A shortcut is a faster way to achieve a result that most often favors expediency over robustness. Sometimes, a shortcut may even involve skipping steps to finish sooner. Shortcuts are, by far, the most common characteristic of avowed lazy programmers. They exalt in the time-saved by their purported cleverness. Here are several specific examples of shortcuts in programming:

a. <u>Brute Force Programming</u>.

This is a general technique of using the computer's brute speed to cover up a poor algorithm choice or poor implementation choice. In the system I am working on, I see this often in the area of custom user interface visualization updates where there is an attitude of "if in doubt, refresh the user interface."

This "refresh always" mentality causes numerous performance drags due to the programmer not willing to take the time to determine whether the interface actually changed but instead just "playing it safe" and refreshing it whether it is needed or not. In our system's case a "refresh" is not free and at times can retrigger a data fetch (very expensive for big data). This is the polar opposite of the "lazy instantiation" or "lazy initialization" technique. The most common examples of brute force programming is in sorting and search. Given that, it is an interesting contrast to know that Donald Knuth's Volume 3 of The Art of Computer Programming is "Sorting and Searching".

Figure 2 Knuth Vol 3

Listing 2 shows the notoriously inefficient "bubble sort" as the canonical example of a brute force algorithm. The hallmark of a brute force technique is that it is the most "straight forward" way of solving the problem and that is where laziness enters the picture. The programmer could not be bothered to consider whether a better approach (in terms of efficiency and effectiveness) was feasible. Now, if this was driven by management schedule pressure, the blame falls with management but many times that is not the case with a "Lazy Programmer" as their laziness overrides the need for a good solution. The attitude that "any solution will do" is often the wrong attitude! On our "big data" system we don't have the luxury of ever assuming a bounded N samples of anything, thus the obvious solution is almost always the wrong one!

Listing 2. Bubble Sort

```
package us.daconta.lazy.programmers.examples;

/**
 * A Lazy Sort
 * @author mdaconta
 */
public class BubbleSorter
{
   static void swap(int [] numArray, int a, int b)
   {
      int tmp = numArray[a];
      numArray[a] = numArray[b];
      numArray[b] = tmp;
   }

   static void bubbleSort(int[] iArray)
   {
      int n = iArray.length;
      int tmp = 0;
      for (int i=0; i < n; i++)
      {
          for (int j=1; j < (n-i); j++)
          {
              if (iArray[j-1] > iArray[j])
              {
                  swap(iArray, j-1, j);
              }
          }
      }
   }
```

```
       }

    public static void main(String [] args)
    {
        try
        {
            int [] testArray = { 20, 2, 88, 44, 33, 51, 99, 4 };
            bubbleSort(testArray);
            for (int i=0; i < testArray.length; i++)
            {
                System.out.println("testArray[" + i + "] is: " + testArray[i]);
            }
        } catch (Throwable t)
        {
            t.printStackTrace();
        }
    }
}
```

Output of the Program is:
testArray[0] is: 2
testArray[1] is: 4
testArray[2] is: 20
testArray[3] is: 33
testArray[4] is: 44
testArray[5] is: 51
testArray[6] is: 88
testArray[7] is: 99

It is important to understand three things here in this criticism of the bubble sort: first, I do not include junior programmers in this criticism as it is expected they would choose the most obvious path (that responsibility thus falls on their team lead to instruct them properly); secondly, it is easy to understand the tantalizing allure of the bubble sort as it is very intuitive. At each step of the loop, you examine the two numbers in front of you and swap the bigger of the two. For small values of N, this is perfectly fine; however, in the age of big data you should never assume small values of N. Finally, using the built-in Arrays.sort() method provides a faster implementation (via the Quicksort algorithm).

 b. Lazy Resource Utilization .

 Similar to "Brute-Force" laziness is a "Resources are free" mindset. By resources, I mean the key computer resources that your program can consume like CPU, memory, threads, network bandwidth and disk space. Computing resources are not infinite and diligent programmers should be good stewards of those resources. Unfortunately, lazy (or naive) programmers are not good stewards of computing resources. Listing 3 is a wasteful implementation of a JDBC Connection. We have seen a similar pattern with network connections, threads, and memory allocations where there is zero consideration of the finite nature of these resources.

Listing 3. Lazy Connection
```
package us.daconta.lazy.programmers.examples;

import java.sql.Connection;
import java.sql.DriverManager;
import java.sql.ResultSet;
import java.sql.SQLException;
import java.sql.Statement;

/**
*
* @author mdaconta
*/
public class LazyConnection {
   private static String url =
     "jdbc:postgresql://localhost:5442/mydb?user=postgres&password=<pwd>!";
   private static boolean initialized=true;
   static {
     try {
       Class.forName("org.postgresql.Driver");
     } catch (ClassNotFoundException ex) {
       System.out.println("Unable to initialive the driver!");
       initialized = false;
```

```
          }
      }

      static class Worker extends Thread {
          public void run() {
              try {
                  Connection con = DriverManager.getConnection(url);
                  Statement stmt = con.createStatement();
                  ResultSet results = stmt.executeQuery("select * from students");
                  while (results.next()) {
                      System.out.println("From Thread " + this.hashCode()
                          + ", Name: " + results.getString(2));
                  }
              } catch (SQLException ex) {
                  System.out.println("Error: " + ex.getMessage() + " ... Abort!");
              }
          }
      }

      public static void main(String [] args) {
          try {
              if (args.length < 1) {
                  System.out.println("USAGE: java LazyConnection <numWorkers>");
                  System.exit(1);
              }

              if (!initialized) {
                  System.out.println("Unable to find the database driver");
              }

              int numWorkers = Integer.parseInt(args[0]);
              for (int i=0; i < numWorkers; i++) {
                  Worker newWorker = new Worker();
                  newWorker.start();
              }
          } catch (Throwable t) {
              t.printStackTrace();
          }
      }
}
```

A run of Listing 3 produces the following output (abridged):

```
From Thread 1784893060, Name: Harry Potter
From Thread 1784893060, Name: Hemione Granger
From Thread 1784893060, Name: Ron Weasley
From Thread 1784893060, Name: Prof. Dumbledore
From Thread 1784893060, Name: Prof. Snapes
From Thread 1784893060, Name: Hagrid
Error: FATAL: sorry, too many clients already ... Abort!
From Thread 247440311, Name: Harry Potter
From Thread 247440311, Name: Hemione Granger
From Thread 247440311, Name: Ron Weasley
From Thread 247440311, Name: Prof. Dumbledore
From Thread 247440311, Name: Prof. Snapes
From Thread 247440311, Name: Hagrid
Error: FATAL: sorry, too many clients already ... Abort!
Error: FATAL: sorry, too many clients already ... Abort!
```

The bottom line here is that connections need pools, memory needs caches and threads need executors. So, in listing 3 we actually have an example of two types of laziness: Connection laziness and Thread laziness. Connection laziness is the poor assumption that when you need a connection you just get another one from the database and don't worry about managing them in your application. As demonstrated here (because we are explicitly not closing them), you can and will run out of database connections. Fortunately, there are many excellent open source Connection pools available to solve this problem so you can manage your application's connections locally and reuse them instead of paying the performance penalty of creating another one.

Listing 3 also has an example of what I call a "thread bomb" brought on by the attitude that "threads are free" (which is a corollary to its evil siblings "memory is free" and "bandwidth is free"). While the program did not run out of threads, they are operating system resources, and you can run out of them. Especially when on a large system with many programs running and thus your program is not the only one creating threads. (Note: the new JVM feature called Fibers[9] will solve this problem by not relying on OS level threads). There are many variants of this type of laziness like "if in doubt, call Refresh()" and "if in doubt, create yet another cache and cache it without any regard to overall memory consumption" and "invent yet another way to do something instead of learning the way others have already done it".

    c. <u>Lazy logging</u>.

This same theme of expediency trumping diligence, can invade the practice of creating debug and error log messages in your code to assist in analyzing a problem. This shortcut involves doing the bare minimum to get by. Such a strategy conforms to the traditional concept of laziness: trying to do a minimal amount of work to just get by. In the area of logging and documentation, such selfishness can hurt a program for years. In fact, lazy logging and poor documentation can deliver "death by a thousand cuts" to a system. Lazy logging means that your logging messages, especially for errors, lack enough information for other developers to understand the problem. In essence, you are doing a disservice to your fellow programmers. Listing 4 demonstrates lazy logging.

Listing 4. Lazy Logger

```
package us.daconta.lazy_programmers;

import java.util.ArrayList;
import java.util.HashMap;
import java.util.List;
import java.util.logging.Level;
import java.util.logging.Logger;

/**
 * Lazy Logger
 *
```

---

[9] https://wiki.openjdk.java.net/display/loom/Main

```
 */
public class LazyLogger
{
  HashMap<String, List<Integer>> classroom =
                new HashMap<String, List<Integer>>();
        Logger logger =
                Logger.getLogger(LazyLogger.class.getCanonicalName());

        /**
         * Add a grade to the students list of grades.
         * @param grade
         *          A student's grade between 0 and 100.
         * @param student
         *          A student's full name.
         */
        public void addGrade(int grade, String student)
        {
          if (null != student && !student.isEmpty())
          {
            List<Integer> grades = classroom.get(student);
            if (null == grades)
            {
              // lazy instantiation (good)
              grades = new ArrayList<Integer>();
            }

            if (grade >= 0 && grade <= 100)
            {
              grades.add(grade);
              classroom.put(student, grades);
            }
            else
            {
              // lazy logging (poor level choice and no context)
              logger.log(Level.ALL, "grade is bad");
              // Better logging
              logger.log(Level.SEVERE, LazyLogger.class.getName(),
                        "addGrade",
                        "The Grade [" + grade + "] for Student [" + student +
                        "] is not between 0 and 100.");
            }
          }
          else
```

```
            {
               // Lazy logging (no context)
               logger.log(Level.SEVERE, "No student.");
               if (null == student)
          {
            // Better logging
            logger.log(Level.SEVERE, "Student input parameter is null.");
          }
          else if (student.isEmpty())
          {
            // Better logging
            logger.log(Level.SEVERE, "Student input parameter is empty.");
          }
        }
      }
}

public static void main( String[] args )
{
    try
    {
      LazyLogger ll = new LazyLogger();
      ll.addGrade(100,null);
      ll.addGrade(100, "");
      ll.addGrade(90, "Mary Smith");
      ll.addGrade(110, "Mary Smith");
    }
    catch (Throwable t)
    {
       t.printStackTrace();
    }
  }
}
```

A run of Listing 4 produces the following results:

Mar 01, 2021 11:10:46 AM us.daconta.lazy_programmers.LazyLogger addGrade
SEVERE: No student.
Mar 01, 2021 11:10:46 AM us.daconta.lazy_programmers.LazyLogger addGrade
SEVERE: Student input parameter is null.
Mar 01, 2021 11:10:46 AM us.daconta.lazy_programmers.LazyLogger addGrade
SEVERE: No student.
Mar 01, 2021 11:10:46 AM us.daconta.lazy_programmers.LazyLogger addGrade

```
SEVERE: Student input parameter is empty.
Mar 01, 2021 11:10:46 AM us.daconta.lazy_programmers.LazyLogger addGrade
SEVERE: The Grade [110] for Student [Mary Smith] is not between 0 and 100.
```

Though a trivial example, what Listing 4 shows is that good logging requires specificity, context and detail.

2. Sweeping problems under the rug.

Unlike the passive laziness of taking shortcuts, this is a more aggressive form of laziness that willfully turns a blind eye to problems. Make no mistake here, at this point laziness is costing you big. Here are three examples of such active laziness:

a. Ignoring code smells.

Have you ever had to counsel a tween that is ignorant of their own body odor? Typically, this is more prevalent among boys right after they reach puberty and have not become used to the additional maintenance chores required by their new states. Well, like teenagers, code can have smells (figuratively) and bad code smells are often ignored by programmers too lazy to clean up the mess! They figure that since they didn't make the mess they are not responsible to clean it up so they ignore the smell.

In Chapter 3 of Martin Fowler's book "Refactoring: Improving the Design of Existing Code", he introduces the concept of code smells (it is worth noting that Kent Beck co-authored the chapter). A code smell is an indication that a body of code is in need of refactoring. Furthermore, refactoring is defined as "a change made to the internal structure of software to make it easier to understand and cheaper to modify without changing its observable behavior."[10]

[10] Fowler, Martin; Refactoring, 2nd Edition; Pg 45.

A bad lazy programmer will ignore these code smells by looking the other way and pretending not to see the litter that is stinking up the code base. Some examples of code smells are duplicated code, long parameter lists, global data, temporary fields and mutable data. Listing 5 demonstrates multiple smells though often times each smell is buried in a larger body of code and thus obscured.

Listing 5. SmellyCode

```
package us.daconta.lazy.programmers.examples;

import java.util.HashMap;

/**
 *
 * @author mdaconta
 */
public class SmellyCode {
    public static int mutableGlobalValue = 120;
    static HashMap<String, Object> appStuff = new HashMap<String, Object>();
    enum ObjectType {typeOne, typeTwo, typeThree};
    ObjectType objectType;

    public void excessivelyLongFunctionNameThatIsARedFlag(int paramOne,
            int paramTwo, Integer paramThree, Double paramFour,
            Object paramFive, int paramSix, long paramSeven, double paramEight,
            int paramTooMany) {
        int value1 = (int) paramOne / paramTwo + paramThree
                        * paramTooMany - paramSix;

        // modifying global values
        mutableGlobalValue = 10;
        appStuff.put("One", paramOne);

        // duplicated code
        int value2 = (int) paramOne / paramTwo + paramThree
                        * paramTooMany - paramSix;

        // tagging a class instead of using subclasses
        objectType = ObjectType.typeOne;
```

```
     // too many if then else statements
     if (paramOne !=100) {
         paramOne = 100;
     } else if (paramOne != 200) {
         paramOne = 200;
     } else if (paramOne != 300) {
         paramOne = 300;
     }
   }
 }
```

Each code smell in Listing 5 is annotated in the comment above it. Some of these are obviously wrong but most just innocently get inserted into a codebase in a casual, almost off-hand manner. But these small infractions accrue over time and add up to big ramifications. Let's use an analogy to demonstrate such impacts. A code base can be thought of as a virtual city where the "broken window theory" is just as relevant to the upkeep of the city as it is to the upkeep of a code base. The "broken window theory" simply states that tolerating even one broken window in a building leads to that building (and eventually the entire block) becoming run-down and dilapidated. In turn, that block's ruin eventually leads to the entire city becoming run-down and dilapidated. All from the small start of a broken window. Why? Because a broken window signifies a lack of concern, a casual attitude that let's small things slip by as if they don't matter. Code smells are the "broken windows" of your code base! They cannot and should not be ignored by lazy programmers! Unfortunately, code smells are just the tip of the iceberg of dangers to your code base from laziness. So, let's dig deeper...

b. Ignoring technical debt.

Moving up the scale of impact and thus seriousness, lazy programmers will ignore technical debt. Really lazy programmers will not only ignore clear technical debt but they will even ignore the reporting of technical debt. Technical debt is the slow accrual of known design flaws into a large code base that increase in cost the longer they are left unfixed (aka unpaid). This metaphor mimics the notion of financial debt in order to highlight that delay in repayment of the debt increases the size of the debt via interest accrual. In essence, not fixing the debt, increases the debt. Of course, we all intuitively know that ignoring a problem does not make it go away, it usually makes it worse. Examples of technical debt are lack of design, complexity creep, misuse of a technique, overuse of a technique and many variants on these themes. Listing 6 demonstrates code with Technical Debt:

Listing 6. TechDebt

```
package us.daconta.lazy.programmers.examples;

import java.awt.image.BufferedImage;
import java.sql.Connection;
import java.sql.DriverManager;
import java.util.HashMap;
import java.util.Random;

/**
 * Brief examples of Technical Debt.
 * @author mdaconta
 */
public class TechDebt {
    /* FIXME - we should really replace this in the future...
       this would be better in a database.
    */
    static HashMap<String, Object> sharedEntities =
                            new HashMap<String, Object>();

    /* BubbleSort - really?  This ARRAY can be HUGE! Junior developer said
       "No time to do this right! So, I copied this from the internet." */
    public static void sortArray(int [] array) {
        for (int i=0; i < array.length; i++) {
            for (int j=1; j < array.length - i; j++) {
                if (array[j-1] > array[j]) {
                    // swap them!
```

```
                int temp = array[j-1];
                array[j-1] = array[j];
                array[j] = temp;
            }
        }
    }
}


    public static void main(String args[]) throws Exception {
        // Initial Load - do these ever get garbage collected?
        for (int i=0; i < Integer.parseInt(args[0]); i++) {
            sharedEntities.put("entity" + i, new BufferedImage(10000, 10000,
                        BufferedImage.TYPE_4BYTE_ABGR));
        }

        // TODO - put this in an encrypted file
        Class.forName("org.postgresql.Driver");
        String dbPassword = "password123";
        String sysUser = "System";
        String url = "jdbc:postgresql://localhost/test";
        Connection conn = DriverManager.getConnection(url, sysUser, dbPassword);

        // create quantities
        Random random = new Random();
        int size = Integer.parseInt(args[1]);
        int [] counts = new int[size];
        for (int i=0; i < size; i++) {
            counts[i] = random.nextInt();
        }
        sortArray(counts);
        System.out.println("Sorted " + counts.length + " items");
    }
}
```

A run of Listing 6 produces:

```
Exception in thread "main" java.lang.OutOfMemoryError: Java heap space
        at java.desktop/java.awt.image.DataBufferByte.<init>(DataBufferByte.java:76)
        at java.desktop/java.awt.image.Raster.createInterleavedRaster(Raster.java:266)
        at java.desktop/java.awt.image.BufferedImage.<init>(BufferedImage.java:391)
        at us.daconta.lazy.programmers.examples.TechDebt.main(TechDebt.java:37)
```

Listing 6 demonstrates several small examples of technical debt that you will see in larger code bases. Typically, the larger the code base the more technical debt you will encounter. In listing 6, we see three examples of technical debt, the use of a large global data structure, an inefficient algorithm choice and an obvious security violation. Of the three, the first one is the most subtle and dangerous because sometimes there are good reasons for a global data structure but in general this is a bad approach. All "global" data goes against the best practice of data encapsulation to protect one classes' data from all other classes. By making data globally accessible you increase the chance of data corruption, memory leaks, and race conditions. This is why in safe languages, like Rust, all data is immutable (unchangeable) by default. The second example of technical debt in Listing 6 is something we covered before in choosing a poor algorithm out of expediency. The developer's excuse of "no time to do it right" is something every technical lead has heard and of which, I have been guilty of in the past. The problem lies not in the initial act which usually has good intentions but of the failure to actually go back and correct it. Does your program have a dedicated "technical debt" team whose full-time job it is to go back and fix technical debt in your system? If not, your code base will degenerate over time. The third example is a serious security violation that happens far more often than anyone would like to admit; however, is so serious that this example of laziness should be grounds for immediate firing. Simply stated, you can never hard-code passwords in your code for convenience. They must be in a secure external file that at a minimum uses the operating system's file protections to protect the file from unauthorized users.

While these are small examples of technical debt, usually a large code base has larger examples of serious technical debt. Some examples of larger technical debt are using a polling approach to implement asynchronous web services (yes, this is an oxymoron but a real example); or having a user interface with four distinct event mechanisms with duplicative functionality; or updating database entities without appropriate locking and thus suffering from the lost update problem. Typically a developer stumbles upon technical debt when something doesn't smell right in the code they are working on. Instead of ignoring their unease, they should go and discuss it with the technical lead. If the technical lead confirms that they have found technical debt they should either see if they can fix it within their current sprint[11] budget or, at a minimum, document it by putting it on the backlog of future work.

c. Failing to create and enforce standards.

As generally intelligent people, most programmers are fiercely independent and like to "go their own way." This programmer characteristic makes creating and enforcing standards difficult at best. I have run multiple standards organizations in my career, both commercially and for the Government, so I understand the difficulties in gaining consensus among smart people. Every programmer in your team or in your project will run across the need for standardization in your coding practices. For example, code formatting, third party libraries, units of measure, data models, git procedures and testing gates. Like code smells, lazy programmers have a tendency to "look the other way" when noticing non-standard behavior in the code. It is very easy to shrug and say, "I didn't create that" or "someone (else) should really fix that". An area of organizational failure is the common failure of enforcing standards across teams when they are being violated. A favorite to ignore is not requiring

---

[11] In Scrum, a sprint is a two-week development cycle. See:
https://en.wikipedia.org/wiki/Scrum_(software_development).

best practices out of fear of thwarting developer creativity. For example, let's say it is agreed upon that all Javascript development should leverage Typescript to achieve strong typing; however, this is not enforced. Thus, time and again, untyped Javascript code enters the baseline with its ensuant risk of dynamic typing. The sad thing here is that a failure to enforce standards is doubly lazy – lazy program management coddling lazy programmers that can't be bothered with a modicum of discipline.

3. **Avoiding architecture**.

The final step in our escalation of bad laziness is the avoidance of architectural concerns in the mad rush to ship new features. Time and again I have heard the same tired old refrain from team leaders that say, "Sorry, that architectural concern (scalability, reliability, security, composability, etc.) is not part of our feature[12]." Oh, really? Well, then just go ahead and focus on your sprint goals and keep your head in the sand. Before we examine specific examples, let us briefly define architecture to "set the stage".

Software Architecture – the design decisions that affect system qualities that we call the "-ilities": Specifically, Reliability, Usability, Scalability, and Extensibility. Reliability enables the system to operate robustly in both common and uncommon conditions (i.e. peak load, extended periods of heavy use, through intermittent failures). Usability enables the system to perform its functions securely and intuitively. Scalability enables the system to handle increasing workloads without significant degradation in performance. Extensibility enables new functions to be easily added to the system. There are other "ilities" (like flexibility) but the ones we discussed

---

[12] In the Scaled Agile Framework, a "feature is a service that fulfills a stakeholder need". See: https://www.scaledagileframework.com/features-and-capabilities/

are the most important. Each of these characteristics flow down from the system level to the component level because each component must do its part in these areas in order to support the system's overall goals.

A common phrase that fits this situation is that a "system is only as strong as its weakest link". The same holds true in architecture. So, like the avoidance of smelly code and technical debt, the avoidance of architectural weakness is usually intentional. What is different than the other types of avoidance is the excuse for the avoidance and the ramifications of such avoidance. The excuse for avoiding architectural weakness is often that the issue is "a system problem that is out of scope of my work". In other words, the excuse is that the issue is "too big to handle now." Unfortunately, the ramification for this avoidance is a massive hole in your architectural qualities that injures not just one part of the system but the entire system! Of course, the argument that a problem is "too big to handle immediately" is very subjective. There are often architectural features that are based on the steady accrual of thousands of techniques that mesh together to create a "bullet-proof" system. Let's look at an example of such a technique that affects system reliability as demonstrated in Listing 7.

Listing 7 RetryConnection

```
package us.daconta.lazy.programmers.examples;

import java.io.IOException;
import java.io.InputStream;
import java.net.URL;

/**
 * Adds retry logic to reading from a URL.
 * Simulates reading from a web service, database or any other server.
 * @author mdaconta
 */
public class RetryConnection {
```

```
public static final int RETRY_WAIT=1000;
public static final int RETRY_ATTEMPTS=5;
public static final int BUFFER_SIZE = 4096;

public String getContent(URL url)
{
   StringBuffer buffer = new StringBuffer();
   int attempts = 0;
   boolean done = false;
   while (!done && attempts++ < RETRY_ATTEMPTS)
   {
      try
      {
         InputStream inputStream = url.openStream();
         int bytesRead = 0;
         byte [] byteArray = new byte[BUFFER_SIZE];
         while ((bytesRead = inputStream.readNBytes(byteArray,
               0, BUFFER_SIZE)) > 0)
         {
            buffer.append(new String(byteArray));
         }
         done = true;
      } catch(IOException ioe)
      {
         System.out.println("ERROR: "
               + ioe.getMessage() + ". Retrying ...");
      }
   }
   return buffer.toString();
}

public static void main(String args[])
{
   try
   {
      if (args.length < 1) {
         System.out.println("Usage: RetryConnection <url>");
         System.exit(1);
      }
      URL url = new URL(args[0]);

      RetryConnection accessor = new RetryConnection();
      System.out.println("Getting content from:" + args[0]);
```

```
        String content = accessor.getContent(url);
        System.out.println("Content:" + content);
    } catch (Throwable t)
      {
        System.out.println("ERROR - Reason: " + t.getLocalizedMessage());
        t.printStackTrace();
      }
  }
}
```

In listing 7, I have implemented a simple, but often overlooked or ignored technique of adding retry logic to communicating with another system component that could either intermittently fail or take longer than expected. This can be coupled with a reasonable timeout period (or even an exponential backoff) so that your code does not wait forever. That is also the reason behind having an "attempt threshold" where you only try so many times (usually at least 3 or more times) before giving up. While the example communicates with a URL, the same retry logic would be useful for communicating with a web service or micro-service. Additionally, this code can be improved by reading the constant values (like RETRY_ATTEMPTS) from a configuration file.

Addressing architectural issues is key to a robust system because they typically affect the system as a whole and not just one team's feature. While listing 7 is a minor example, I have witnessed numerous larger examples of architectural avoidance. Three such examples are hogging resources, shifting the workload (and blame) to other parts of the system, and not-invented-here syndrome. If you are working on a component that is IO bound, there is always a temptation to create a local memory cache to avoid frequent re-fetching. While this is a good strategy for your component, it can be a bad strategy for the overall program or system.

I have seen examples where the same data was cached multiple times due to short-sighted developers not knowing another component had already cached the same data. Rogue caches, rogue executors, rogue connection pools, rogue properties, rogue files and even rogue database tables often follow the same pattern: short-term convenience that causes long-term maintenance problems. While it should be obvious, shared resources require big-picture thinking, not myopic thinking.

The second example is when a component shifts a burden to another system component (like the database) or another service. I have seen this many times where poorly constructed queries or "one-over-the-world" queries are sent to the database and then the results are filtered locally (in memory) by the component. While it may "work" in the short-run or when the database tables are small (like often occurs on test systems), it is a ticking time bomb when the system goes into production. While sometimes these blatant examples of poor practice cause a good laugh, they also are variants of robbing Peter to pay Paul. Pay specific attention to any queries that retrieve "all records"[13] of one or more tables. You may say, "No one would be that stupid"... and you would be wrong.

Our final example of architectural avoidance, "not invented here" involves the double-edged sword of distrust. There are times when distrusting other's code is warranted but that should be the exception and not the rule. Too many times, I have seen developers re-invent the wheel instead of reusing existing code in the system that does the same or similar function. Now, sometimes this is a failure of training because a developer may not be aware that a good alternative already exists. Unfortunately, lazy programmers often have

---

[13] Or all fields. "All" being the red flag.

an itchy trigger finger when they see that implementing it "quickly" in "their way" is faster then learning how someone else did it. This is especially true if data needs to be transformed or the API may not be precisely what is required. Such, simple "off by a little" scenarios should not be excuses to re-implement the code "in your 'better' way" but instead be opportunities to improve the system-wide utility for the benefit of the entire program.

To recap, we have covered three categories of bad-lazy techniques: taking shortcuts, sweeping dirt under the rug, and avoiding architecture. So, how do you avoid all of the "bad lazy" techniques we covered in this chapter? The first step is to be cognizant that every programmer, including yourself, will be faced with the temptation to take the expedient path. So, knowing what not to do is just as important as knowing what to do. Furthermore, being aware of these temptations will help you police your peers and assist your team leader in creating quality code. This does take courage to carry out. It takes courage to push back against schedule pressure. It takes courage to tactfully confront another developer about their coding habits. And finally, it takes courage to refactor code to support architectural goals. So, do the right thing and not the expedient thing.

Chapter 4 The Ugly

The last chapter covered multiple ways that "laziness" in programming conforms to its traditional definition of work avoidance. We examined, in detail, multiple practices that "muddy" the code base and litter it with technical debt. In this chapter we will discuss the ramifications of these techniques on a large program over time. In my career, I have been called in multiple times to rescue failing programs from the verge of cancellation. After digging into the problems the root causes always turned out to be the same: poor design, poor practices and poor attitudes. Miraculously, after you clean up the first two; the third usually improves on its own! In this chapter we will examine three "ugly" consequences of those "Bad Lazy" practices we discussed in the previous chapter.

1. **Destroying Architectural Cohesion.**

Avoiding code smells, avoiding technical debt and avoiding architecture has serious consequences for your code base. Over time, your cohesive software system will degenerate into a "Big Ball of Mud"[14] As defined by the coiners of the term (Brian Foote and Joseph Yoder) a big ball of mud is "a haphazardly structured, sprawling, sloppy, duct-tape-and-baling-wire, spaghetti-code jungle. These systems show unmistakable signs of unregulated growth, and repeated, expedient repair."

---

[14] "Big Ball of Mud", paper by Brian Foote and Joseph Yoder, 1997.
https://joeyoder.com/PDFs/mud.pdf

We have known about the dangers of goto statements, spaghetti code and software entropy for many years. Beginning with Dijkstra's famous letter to the editor of ACM, "Go To Statement Considered Harmful"[15], there have been numerous warnings against the entropic slide of software as it ages. The complexity of the software increases, the band-aids get put atop older band-aids, and more programmers shrug their shoulders at all the broken windows.

But is this the fate of all software? No, as is contrasted in Figure 3. It is important to understand the difference between these two diagrams and how Lazy programmers contribute to the latter case.

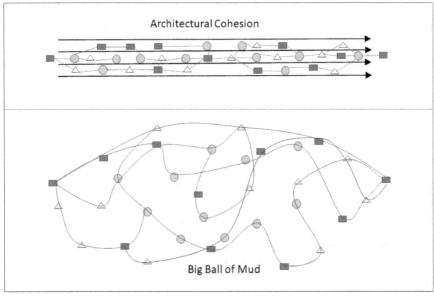

Figure 3 Destroying Architectural Cohesion

Figure 3 has two diagrams, the first demonstrating a system with strong architectural cohesion and the second demonstrating how a system loses that cohesion and

[15] "Go-to statement considered harmful", Edsger W. Dijkstra; 1968.

degenerates into a big ball of mud. Let's begin with the top diagram where a system has strong architectural cohesion between its components. What does this mean?

It means the components know where they fit into the overall system and they "stay within their lane". A well-behaved component does its function efficiently, effectively and with good test coverage. A well-behaved component does not shift its burden to other components and gracefully handles both peak loads and error conditions (like network latency, storage failures, out of memory exceptions and other exceptions). A well-behaved component has "clean lines" and carries out its task in the simplest manner possible. Going back to our definition of a big ball of mud we see the word "expedient repair" as a chief culprit in the degeneration of the software. The rules of a well-behaved component are frequently violated in the name of "expediency". Schedule pressure is the "go to" excuse of the Lazy Programmer. The next favorite excuse is "efficiency" but by efficiency they mean "their efficiency" and not the code's efficiency. In other words, labor-saving techniques for their personal benefit and not necessarily for the project's benefit. Every expedient solution to a problem leads directly to a shortcut which should be thought of as a cut on the architecture. A cut between the lines. A cut into the "design muscles" of the system. And the system staggers which leads to more emergency repairs which leads to more expediency and more cuts. This is the meaning of the phrase, "death by a thousand cuts".

Of course, this slow degeneration of a system can take years. The only way to fix it is to have the courage to clean up the technical debt and to ruthlessly refactor those rogue components. How do you know if your System is moving in the right or wrong direction? By monitoring and measuring whether it regresses when adding new features.

2. **Slipping into System Regression**.

A software system evolves via a continuous stream of enhancements to satisfy user requirements. Each "careless cut" placed in the system by a lazy programmer weakens that part of the system. For example, lazy comments make it harder for another programmer to understand the code. Lazy logging makes it harder to diagnose errors. Sloppy resource utilization stresses multiple parts of the system simultaneously which causes cascading errors. When symptoms cascade to other symptoms they become far removed from the root cause of the problem. And as the root cause festers, parts of the system that worked previously can suddenly fail (or collapse from strain as in Figure 4).

Figure 4 System Regression Analogy[16]

A system regression typically follows the proverbial "one step forward, two steps back". In concrete terms, the software system regresses when a feature added to one part of the system breaks another part of the system. Now, let's cover

---

[16] Image from Bishnu Sarangi on Pixabay.com and free for commercial use. https://pixabay.com/photos/bridge-collapse-damage-312873/

how to prevent this from happening through robust, automated regression tests.

Regression testing can be performed in a manual approach (via a functional tester) and in an automated fashion via unit tests for the backend and User Interface robots for the front-end. In the context of Lazy programming, we are only concerned with the creation of unit tests by software developers as part of their normal development process. If programmers are most concerned about saving time or finishing as soon as possible (possibly due to schedule pressure), then testing can be an afterthought. In contrast, proponents of Test-Driven Development (TDD) recommend writing the tests first. The real danger in writing unit tests is to treat them like a checkbox that just needs to be done for each new class or method that you created. This "checkbox approach" is only concerned about finishing and not at all concerned about how to write tests well. So, let's focus the next example on how to test to insure you cover edge cases and corner cases. An edge case focuses on one variable on the extreme end of a boundary (aka "the edge"). A corner case focuses on more than one variable (in the same way that a corner is the intersection of two boundaries).

Listing 8 sets the stage for our unit tests by offering a simple but common case in need of good testing: validating the input parameters to a method. Listing 8 is a simple program to load an image into a frame with a method to generate a sub-image given a rectangle. (Note: since this example is long, it is condensed here and the full source code listing is in Appendix 2).

Listing 8. ImageTool
```
package us.daconta.lazy.programmers.examples;

// ... imports removed for brevity, See Appendix 2
```

```java
/**
 * @author mdaconta
 */
public class ImageTool extends JFrame
{
    private BufferedImage image;
    public ImageTool(String fullpath) throws IOException
    {
        this(new ImageIcon(fullpath));
    }

    // ... Constructors and helper methods removed for brevity – see Appendix 2
    // *key method* we want to test carefully is below ...
    public BufferedImage getSubImage(Rectangle r)
    {
        BufferedImage subImage = null;
        if (image != null)
        {
            Rectangle imgRect = new Rectangle(0, 0, image.getWidth(),
                                                    image.getHeight());
            if (r != null && imgRect.contains(r))
            {
                subImage = image.getSubimage(r.x, r.y, r.width, r.height);
            }
        }
        return subImage;
    }

    public static void main(String [] args)
    {
        try
        {
            ImageTool imgFrame = new ImageTool(args[0]);
            imgFrame.setVisible(true);
            int x = Integer.parseInt(args[1]);
            int y = Integer.parseInt(args[2]);
            int width = Integer.parseInt(args[3]);
            int height = Integer.parseInt(args[4]);
            BufferedImage subImage = imgFrame.getSubImage(new
                                            Rectangle(x,y,width,height));
            ImageTool subImageFrame = new ImageTool(subImage);
            subImageFrame.setVisible(true);
        } catch (Throwable t)
```

```
      {
        t.printStackTrace();
      }
   }
}
```

To write good unit tests for the ImageTool class, you need to write tests for each non-trivial method (unlike getters and setters or other methods with no input parameters). For this example, let's focus on just one method, getSubImage(), which takes a single parameter a Rectangle that represents the section of the original image you want to "extract" into a new image. The way to think about unit testing is to focus on five different types of test cases: the common case, the boundary case, the existence case, the empty case and other data-type specific variants. The bottom line is that writing good tests is hard. You must think about each of these cases and come up with a test for each variant.

For our unit test, we need to think about all those cases in relation to the input data (a rectangle), the source data and the resulting sub-image. While this example is simple, it offers some insight into the more generic case of checking for containment of a smaller entity. It also represents an easy way to visualize edge cases and corner cases. Listing 9 presents eleven tests for the getSubImage() method.

Listing 9. ImageToolTest
```
package us.daconta.lazy.programmers.examples;

// imports removed for brevity

/**
 * JUnit tests for ImageTool class.
 * @author mdaconta
 */
public class ImageToolTest {
```

```
private boolean comparePixels(BufferedImage image1, BufferedImage image2) {
   int width = image1.getWidth();
   int height = image1.getHeight();
   int width2 = image2.getWidth();
   int height2 = image2.getHeight();
   if (width != width2 || height != height2) {
      return false;
   }

   for (int row = 0; row < height; row++) {
      for (int col = 0; col < width; col++) {
         if (image1.getRGB(col,row) != image2.getRGB(col,row))
         {
            return false;
         }
      }
   }
   return true;
}
/**
 * Test of getSubImage method, of class ImageTool.
 */
@org.junit.jupiter.api.Test
public void testGetSubImage() throws IOException {
   System.out.println("Testing getSubImage");
   ImageTool instance = new ImageTool(
      "C:\\Users\\mdaconta\\Documents\\ paycheck-programmer.jpg");
   BufferedImage image = instance.getImage();
   System.out.println("Test #1: null");
   Rectangle r = null;
   BufferedImage expResult = null;
   BufferedImage result = instance.getSubImage(r);
   assertEquals(expResult, result);

   /* Note: these would all be separately viewed and validated against a known
      image for correctness or even better, generated programmatically in a
      standard, synthetic test pattern. */
   BufferedImage upperEdge = image.getSubimage(0, 0, image.getWidth(), 1);
   BufferedImage lowerEdge = image.getSubimage(0, image.getHeight() - 1,
                                          image.getWidth(),1);
   BufferedImage rightEdge = image.getSubimage(image.getWidth() - 1, 0, 1,
                                          image.getHeight());
   BufferedImage leftEdge = image.getSubimage(0, 0, 1, image.getHeight());
```

```
BufferedImage upperLeftCorner = image.getSubimage(0, 0, 1, 1);
BufferedImage upperRightCorner = image.getSubimage(image.getWidth() - 1,
                                                    0, 1, 1);
BufferedImage lowerLeftCorner = image.getSubimage(0, image.getHeight() -
                                                    1, 1, 1);
BufferedImage lowerRightCorner = image.getSubimage(image.getWidth() - 1,
                                                    image.getHeight() - 1, 1, 1);

System.out.println("Test #2: zeroes");
r = new Rectangle(0,0,0,0);
expResult = null;
result = instance.getSubImage(r);
assertEquals(expResult, result);

System.out.println("Test #3: negative");
r = new Rectangle(-1,1,1,1);
expResult = null;
result = instance.getSubImage(r);
assertEquals(expResult, result);

// upper edge
System.out.println("Test #4: upper edge");
r = new Rectangle(0,0,image.getWidth(),1);
int expectedWidth = image.getWidth();
int expectedHeight = 1;
result = instance.getSubImage(r);
assertResults(result, upperEdge, expectedWidth, expectedHeight);

// ...Tests 5 – 10  are eliminated here for brevity,  See Appendix 2

// LR corner
System.out.println("Test #11: LR corner");
r = new Rectangle(image.getWidth() - 1, image.getHeight() - 1, 1, 1);
expectedWidth = 1;
expectedHeight = 1;
result = instance.getSubImage(r);
assertResults(result, lowerRightCorner, expectedWidth, expectedHeight);
}

private void assertResults(BufferedImage result, BufferedImage expectedResult,
            int expectedWidth, int expectedHeight)
{
    assertNotNull(result);
```

```
    assertEquals(result.getWidth(), expectedWidth);
    assertEquals(result.getHeight(), expectedHeight);
    assertTrue(comparePixels(result, expectedResult));
  }
}
```

As you can see in Listing 9, we use eleven tests to provide proper test coverage of the existence test (null), numeric tests (0 and negative), the edge cases and corner cases. Another important reason to test edge cases is to prevent "Off-By-One" errors. Off-by-one errors most often occur at the edges. Finally, you should take note of the various helper methods (i.e. comparePixels() and assertResults() to improve the tests). To complete the example, Listing 10 is the maven run of the test results.

Listing 10. Maven Run of Junit Tests

--- maven-surefire-plugin:2.12.4:test (default-test) @ lazy-programmers-examples ---

Surefire report directory: C:\Users\mdaconta\Documents\NetBeansProjects\lazy-programmers-examples\target\surefire-reports

```
-------------------------------------------------------
 T E S T S
-------------------------------------------------------
Running us.daconta.lazy.programmers.examples.ImageToolTest
Testing getSubImage
Test #1: null
Test #2: zeroes
Test #3: negative
Test #4: upper edge
Test #5: lower edge
Test #6: left edge
Test #7: right edge
Test #8: UL corner
Test #9: UR corner
Test #10: LL corner
Test #11: LR corner
Tests run: 1, Failures: 0, Errors: 0, Skipped: 0, Time elapsed: 0.307 sec
```

Results :

Tests run: 1, Failures: 0, Errors: 0, Skipped: 0

As we stated before, edge cases and corner cases are hard! Lazy programmers are typically only concerned about coverage, not the quality of their tests. Checking boxes gives your team and the program at large a false sense of confidence.

One final piece of advice in regard to unit testing is that whenever a bug in the software is found, you should immediately write a unit test that both demonstrates the bug and proves that when it is fixed, it is fixed forever. Of course, that will be the case because your unit test will always test for it, in every new iteration of the software.

3. **Most Lazy programmers are paycheck programmers**.

At what point does a programmer's desire to find an easier way become an excuse for avoiding the hard tasks (like design)? At what point does automating drudgery become blinders to tasks that are worth drudging through (like tedious edge cases in unit tests)?

I have seen the mantle of "good laziness" used as a badge of honor to conceal a basic lack of discipline – as if development should be easy, as if development should be fast, as if the programmer cannot bear the weight of a time-consuming task. While the result of this is an expedient solution, the motivation for that expediency is simply the paycheck. In other words, the project's objectives are secondary to the paycheck. The mission of the project or the mission that the project supports is tangential to "just another day at the factory".

Figure 5 A Paycheck Programmer[17]

Figure 5 depicts a paycheck programmer who always chooses the pay over the mission. Of course, this is not often a conscious choice and that is actually the most dangerous aspect of this weakness. Operating as a "default setting" to choose expediency over quality is part and parcel of the human condition. It is a perennial temptation that we all must deal with. As a veteran of the Military, I have always operated under a strong sense of mission at the expense of personal comfort. The military works hard at instilling this characteristic into the profession. That, of course, begs the question of just what is a profession, what is a professional and how does your definition of "laziness" affect that?

A profession[18] is an occupation that requires specialized skills and practices, an established body of

---

knowledge, and a community of practitioners to enforce the standards and ethics in the field. A profession usually emerges over time as a specialized trade craft evolves into a profession. It takes time for a group of practitioners to understand their craft, codify its best practices and then promulgate those practices to its adherents. Software development, also known as Software Engineering in some circles, has been evolving and maturing since the inception of widely adopted "high-level"[19] programming languages in the 1950's. Given that as a starting point, the trade craft of building computer programs has been evolving and maturing for seventy years. Many practitioners, including myself, believe that our body of knowledge, practices and ethics have matured to the point where we are ready to move from a craft to a profession. Right now, this is a question that concerns every software developer and begs the question: "Are we ready to become Software Engineering Professionals?" Are you ready? Should we be ready, as a group of practitioners, to take the next step?

In 2011, Marc Andreesen penned an op-ed in the Wall Street Journal entitled "Why Software is Eating the World"[20]. The article highlighted a new reality in the economics of business whereby all companies have become increasingly reliant on the software that runs their business. For example, car companies are now becoming software companies because so many of the car's components are controlled by software. Many industries are becoming disrupted by software like publishing, telecommunications, retail stores, banking, movies and cable companies. What does this mean for software developers? The software you create is affecting more and more people, which raises the urgency of our industry transforming from a trade craft into a profession. The

---

[19] https://en.wikipedia.org/wiki/History_of_programming_languages
[20] https://a16z.com/2011/08/20/why-software-is-eating-the-world/

practitioners of a profession are expected to act like a "professional" at all times.

Professionalism is a defined code of conduct by the practitioners of a profession. For software engineers, the most well known code of ethics and conduct is the one developed by the Association of Computing Machinery (ACM) and reprinted as Appendix 1 (in accordance with their permission statement). Simply stated, I believe that laziness as defined and demonstrated in Chapter 3 violates section 2.1 of our Professional Responsibilities which states: "Strive to achieve high quality in both the processes and products of professional work." So, to put this bluntly, lazy programmers lack professionalism.

Team leaders need to be keenly aware of this. My plea to those who lead software teams is this: "Don't turn your team into paycheck programmers by promulgating 'laziness as a virtue'". Instead, stress that you have to be willing to struggle through difficult things. Struggle with design. Struggle with the architectural issues. Struggle through troubleshooting and debugging. The hard reality that we accept is this: quality code is not supposed to be easy.

In the end, supporting the mission of our end-users is the most important thing. Crafting code that is useful. Getting the code into hands of the users to better their lives. Code that performs the purpose it was designed for and performs it well. As professionals, we take pride in our performance, our software products, and their role in shaping the future.

Chapter 5 Conclusion

In this book we have examined the good side, the bad side, and the ugly ramifications of "lazy programming". Let's briefly recap some of the key points and then answer the "so what" questions we posed in the introduction. In Chapter 2, **The Good**, we introduced three ways that lazy programming can be "good":

1. Lazy can mean "efficient".
2. Lazy can mean "creative".
3. Lazy coding techniques are part of the vernacular.

While all these techniques are good practices that should not be dismissed, the problem lies in attaching the term "lazy" to them. Automating repetitive tasks can just as easily be labeled "strategic effort" instead of "lazy". There are plenty of phrases in common language like "penny wise and pound foolish" that refer to the concept of long-term, strategic thinking (or effort). In regards to the "creative laziness" of finding an easy way to do "hard things", it can just as easily be accounted for by simple evolution of our craft. Finally, the coding techniques explicitly defined as "lazy" like "Lazy Instantiation or Lazy Initialization", are simply anthropomorphizing our software in a tongue-in-cheek fashion. A more accurate description would be "just-in-time" or "As Necessary". Poor language use is simply that and nothing more.

In Chapter 3, **The Bad**, we examined three categories (with multiple examples in each) of traditional lazy behavior:

1. Shortcuts and Band-Aids.

2. Sweeping Problems Under the Rug.
3. Avoiding Architectural Issues.

These are serious issues that we demonstrated with concrete examples from hard-won, real-life experience. Taking shortcuts in the name of expediency is by far the most common poor practice. The excuse of "not enough time to do it right" is pervasive and sometimes even true. This practice is so common because it comes from two directions, lazy programmers and short-sighted managers. Ignoring code smells and technical debt is rationalized away as "not my problem". On one end of the spectrum, a code smell is ignored as "just a little messiness that is not a big deal"; whereas technical debt is seen as "too big to tackle right now". Both answers are clear signs of both poor training (or no training) and poor code reviews when checking-in code. Team-wide technical code reviews are critical to train your team members on both "what-to-do" and "what-not-to-do"! Finally, avoiding architectural issues is the worst variant of a problem seeming to be "too big to handle right now." Unfortunately, it also has the most serious ramifications for the long-term health of the project.

In Chapter 4, **The Ugly**, we revealed and demonstrated three ramifications of the lazy practices of Chapter 3:

1. Destroying Architectural Cohesion.
2. Slipping into System Regression.
3. Most Lazy Programmers are Paycheck Programmers.

A truism in many areas of life is that avoiding problems never works because the problems fester and grow until they are too big to ignore. This is the fate of every carefully designed software system if expediency trumps quality. In chapter three's final section, we described software architecture in terms of the characteristics (reliability, security, scalability, etc.) that the system was designed to achieve. If those design decisions are not adhered to then the system's architectural cohesion will diminish. While this can again generally be blamed on schedule pressures, it is worth noting that Agile processes that are very much in vogue today tend to short-change design (especially BDUF[21]).

Regression testing is a mainstay of good testing practices so that a project continually improves. If a system regresses, it means that adding new features breaks old features. This is a cardinal sin for a project and strong evidence that your team has allowed bad habits to slip into their routine. Laziness in creating automated tests is a major contributor to system regression and this section took pains to demonstrate how to thoroughly test code. We demonstrated four types of test cases: existence, data-type specific, edge cases and corner cases. Unfortunately, lazy programmers tend to ignore testing edge cases and corner cases for the easier "common case". As I have stated many times in this book, these programmers will rationalize this due to schedule pressure. Though not the subject of this book, I have witnessed the Scrum development process, with its focus on two-week "sprints", encourage such short-term thinking. If you only think in terms of two weeks, it is easy to focus only on the "trees" in front of you and miss the forest.

The end of Chapter 4 opened the aperture to address the ramification of "lazy programming" to the software profession as a whole and to the professionalism of its practitioners. I strongly asserted that lazy programmers are "paycheck programmers" because they care more for the paycheck then the mission. By mission, I mean the benefit of the software to the end-users. In some ways we have come full

---

[21] https://en.wikipedia.org/wiki/Big_Design_Up_Front

circle because in the introduction of this book we compared it to Ayn Rand's book the "Virtue of Selfishness". In fact, I am asserting that Lazy Programmers subscribe to that vision. "Laziness as a virtue" is the same puerile nonsense once espoused by Mark Zuckerberg with Facebook's motto, "move fast and break things". Such immature thought has no place in a society where software is "eating the world", driverless cars are on our roads, and AI algorithms surveil the public spaces.

We are now prepared to answer the questions we posed in the introduction of this book:

- "For skill development and the furtherance of your career, is Laziness a Virtue or Vice?"

  If you remove semantics from this question and just focus on the behaviors, the answer becomes clear. Furthering your skillset requires effort and the right mindset, so anything that seeks to skirt effort or avoid work will not help you improve your technical skills. To have longevity in the technical field, you must be willing to continually learn new things, challenge yourself and teach the things you know to your fellow programmers. The traditional definition of lazy violates the principles of conduct clearly laid out in the ACM Code of Ethics and Professional Conduct (reprinted in Appendix 1).

- "For a team leader, should you develop 'Laziness' in your junior developers or squash it like a bad habit?"

  Here we are again faced with a conundrum as to the right approach due to the legitimacy of some of the techniques discussed in Chapter 2. Thus, in the same way a good parent struggles over disciplining a child so as to help and not hinder their growth, a good team leader will struggle over exerting discipline upon team members. The best way to do this is to separate the attitude from the actions. In other words, it is good to encourage originality and labor-saving efforts to reduce repetitive tasks. At the same time, it is important to remain vigilant against taking shortcuts, avoiding difficult tasks (i.e. technical debt, architecture, etc.) and deficient testing. The ramifications of "bad laziness" are too severe to allow a lazy attitude, in any form, to exist unchallenged by the team leader. As Thomas More said "Silence gives consent". Thus, a team leader must not remain silent on this important issue.

- "For the profession of programming as an engineering discipline, does 'Laziness' enhance or reduce the respect our profession garners from society at large?"

This question is by far the easiest as you will be hard-pressed to find "laziness" in any professional code of conduct. And if you do happen to find one, please email me so I can avoid that profession at all costs. A simple thought experiment will prove this point: would you seek medical care from a physician that professed to "lazy diagnoses"? Of course not and the same is true for the software engineering profession. Unfortunately, lazy practitioners are not the real problem in elevating software engineering to the status of a "profession". Free market proponents fear licensing of programmers will "kill the golden goose" and disrupt this growth industry. Simultaneously, regulators struggle with the nascency of the industry and the very nature of "software" (in contrast to hardware). Thus, it is the responsibility of every practitioner to make it clear that our profession has matured to the point where we know how to create reliable software and should be held accountable (via licensing) to do so. I, for one, am a strong proponent of the licensing of software engineers. I would acquire a license to practice in this field.

In closing, I encourage every practitioner to read and follow the ACM code of ethics and professional conduct printed in Appendix 1. To that code of conduct, I would add conduct specifically related to laziness. Something like this:

"As a Professional Software Engineer, I will not practice, promote or promulgate any behavior that seeks to avoid work to the detriment of the long-term success of the project. I will not ignore code smells, technical debt or architectural issues for the sake of expediency. I will support the mission of our end-users by striving, at all times, to deliver high quality software. Furthermore, I will request the same discipline and vigilance from other members of my team and ask they do the same for me."

Appendix 1 ACM Code of Ethics

ACM Code of Ethics and Professional Conduct

Preamble

Computing professionals' actions change the world. To act responsibly, they should reflect upon the wider impacts of their work, consistently supporting the public good. The ACM Code of Ethics and Professional Conduct ("the Code") expresses the conscience of the profession.

The Code is designed to inspire and guide the ethical conduct of all computing professionals, including current and aspiring practitioners, instructors, students, influencers, and anyone who uses computing technology in an impactful way. Additionally, the Code serves as a basis for remediation when violations occur. The Code includes principles formulated as statements of responsibility, based on the understanding that the public good is always the primary consideration. Each principle is supplemented by guidelines, which provide explanations to assist computing professionals in understanding and applying the principle.

Section 1 outlines fundamental ethical principles that form the basis for the remainder of the Code. Section 2 addresses additional, more specific considerations of professional responsibility. Section 3 guides individuals who have a leadership role, whether in the workplace or in a volunteer professional capacity. Commitment to ethical conduct is required of every ACM member, and principles involving compliance with the Code are given in Section 4.

The Code as a whole is concerned with how fundamental ethical principles apply to a computing professional's conduct. The Code is not an algorithm for solving ethical problems; rather it serves as a basis for ethical decision-making. When thinking through a particular issue, a computing professional may find that multiple principles should be taken into account, and that different principles will have different relevance to the issue.

Questions related to these kinds of issues can best be answered by thoughtful consideration of the fundamental ethical principles, understanding that the public good is the paramount consideration. The entire computing profession benefits when the ethical decision-making process is accountable to and transparent to all stakeholders. Open discussions about ethical issues promote this accountability and transparency.

1. GENERAL ETHICAL PRINCIPLES.

A computing professional should...

1.1 Contribute to society and to human well-being, acknowledging that all people are stakeholders in computing.

This principle, which concerns the quality of life of all people, affirms an obligation of computing professionals, both individually and collectively, to use their skills for the benefit of society, its members, and the environment surrounding them. This obligation includes promoting fundamental human rights and protecting each individual's right to autonomy. An essential aim of computing professionals is to minimize negative consequences of computing, including threats to health, safety, personal security, and privacy. When the interests of multiple groups conflict, the needs of those less advantaged should be given increased attention and priority.

Computing professionals should consider whether the results of their efforts will respect diversity, will be used in socially responsible ways, will meet social needs, and will be broadly accessible. They are encouraged to actively contribute to society by engaging in pro bono or volunteer work that benefits the public good.

In addition to a safe social environment, human well-being requires a safe natural environment. Therefore, computing professionals should promote environmental sustainability both locally and globally.

1.2 Avoid harm.

In this document, "harm" means negative consequences, especially when those consequences are significant and unjust. Examples of harm include unjustified physical or mental injury, unjustified destruction or disclosure of information, and unjustified damage to property, reputation, and the environment. This list is not exhaustive.

Well-intended actions, including those that accomplish assigned duties, may lead to harm. When that harm is unintended, those responsible are obliged to undo or mitigate the harm as much as possible. Avoiding harm begins with careful consideration of potential impacts on all those affected by decisions. When harm is an intentional part of the system, those responsible are obligated to ensure that the harm is ethically justified. In either case, ensure that all harm is minimized.

To minimize the possibility of indirectly or unintentionally harming others, computing professionals should follow generally accepted best practices unless there is a compelling ethical reason to do otherwise. Additionally, the consequences of data aggregation and emergent properties of systems should be carefully analyzed. Those involved with pervasive or infrastructure systems should also consider Principle 3.7.

A computing professional has an additional obligation to report any signs of system risks that might result in harm. If leaders do not act to curtail or mitigate such risks, it may be necessary to "blow the whistle" to reduce potential harm. However, capricious or misguided reporting of risks can itself be harmful. Before reporting risks, a computing professional should carefully assess relevant aspects of the situation.

1.3 Be honest and trustworthy.

Honesty is an essential component of trustworthiness. A computing professional should be transparent and provide full disclosure of all pertinent system capabilities, limitations, and potential problems to the appropriate parties. Making deliberately false or misleading claims, fabricating or falsifying data, offering or accepting bribes, and other dishonest conduct are violations of the Code.

Computing professionals should be honest about their qualifications, and about any limitations in their competence to complete a task. Computing professionals should be forthright about any circumstances that might lead to either real or perceived conflicts of interest or otherwise tend to undermine the independence of their judgment. Furthermore, commitments should be honored.

Computing professionals should not misrepresent an organization's policies or procedures, and should not speak on behalf of an organization unless authorized to do so.

1.4 Be fair and take action not to discriminate.

The values of equality, tolerance, respect for others, and justice govern this principle. Fairness requires that even careful decision processes provide some avenue for redress of grievances.

Computing professionals should foster fair participation of all people, including those of underrepresented groups. Prejudicial discrimination on the basis of age, color, disability, ethnicity, family status, gender identity, labor union membership, military status, nationality, race, religion or belief, sex, sexual orientation, or any other inappropriate factor is an explicit violation of the Code. Harassment, including sexual harassment, bullying, and other abuses of power and authority, is a form of discrimination that, amongst other harms, limits fair access to the virtual and physical spaces where such harassment takes place.

The use of information and technology may cause new, or enhance existing, inequities. Technologies and practices should be as inclusive and accessible as possible and computing professionals should take action to avoid creating systems or technologies that disenfranchise or oppress people. Failure to design for inclusiveness and accessibility may constitute unfair discrimination.

1.5 Respect the work required to produce new ideas, inventions, creative works, and computing artifacts.

Developing new ideas, inventions, creative works, and computing artifacts creates value for society, and those who expend this effort should expect to gain value from their work. Computing professionals should therefore credit the creators of ideas, inventions, work, and artifacts, and respect copyrights, patents, trade secrets, license agreements, and other methods of protecting authors' works.

Both custom and the law recognize that some exceptions to a creator's control of a work are necessary for the public good. Computing professionals should not unduly oppose reasonable uses of their intellectual works. Efforts to help others by contributing time and energy to projects that help society illustrate a positive aspect of this principle. Such efforts include free and open source software and work put into the public domain. Computing professionals should not claim private ownership of work that they or others have shared as public resources.

1.6 Respect privacy.

The responsibility of respecting privacy applies to computing professionals in a particularly profound way. Technology enables the collection, monitoring, and exchange of personal information quickly, inexpensively, and often without the knowledge of the people affected. Therefore, a computing professional should become conversant in the various definitions and forms of privacy and should understand the rights and responsibilities associated with the collection and use of personal information.

Computing professionals should only use personal information for legitimate ends and without violating the rights of individuals and groups. This requires taking precautions to prevent re-identification of anonymized data or unauthorized data collection, ensuring the accuracy of data, understanding the provenance of the data, and protecting it from unauthorized access and accidental disclosure. Computing professionals should establish transparent policies and procedures that allow individuals to understand what data is being collected and how it is being used, to give informed consent for automatic data collection, and to review, obtain, correct inaccuracies in, and delete their personal data.

Only the minimum amount of personal information necessary should be collected in a system. The retention and disposal periods for that information should be clearly defined, enforced, and communicated to data subjects. Personal information gathered for a specific purpose should not be used for other purposes without the person's consent. Merged data collections can compromise privacy features present in the original collections. Therefore, computing professionals should take special care for privacy when merging data collections.

1.7 Honor confidentiality.

Computing professionals are often entrusted with confidential information such as trade secrets, client data, nonpublic business strategies, financial information, research data, pre-publication scholarly articles, and patent applications. Computing professionals should protect confidentiality except in cases where it is evidence of the violation of law, of organizational regulations, or of the Code. In these cases, the nature or contents of that information should not be disclosed except to appropriate authorities. A computing professional should consider thoughtfully whether such disclosures are consistent with the Code.

2. PROFESSIONAL RESPONSIBILITIES.

A computing professional should...

2.1 Strive to achieve high quality in both the processes and products of professional work.

Computing professionals should insist on and support high quality work from themselves and from colleagues. The dignity of employers, employees, colleagues, clients, users, and anyone else affected either directly or indirectly by the work should be respected throughout the process. Computing professionals should respect the right of those involved to transparent communication about the project. Professionals should be cognizant of any serious negative consequences affecting any stakeholder that may result from poor quality work and should resist inducements to neglect this responsibility.

2.2 Maintain high standards of professional competence, conduct, and ethical practice.

High quality computing depends on individuals and teams who take personal and group responsibility for acquiring and maintaining professional competence. Professional competence starts with technical knowledge and with awareness of the social context in which their work may be deployed. Professional competence also requires skill in communication, in reflective analysis, and in recognizing and navigating ethical challenges. Upgrading skills should be an ongoing process and might include independent study, attending conferences or seminars, and other informal or formal education. Professional organizations and employers should encourage and facilitate these activities.

2.3 Know and respect existing rules pertaining to professional work.

"Rules" here include local, regional, national, and international laws and regulations, as well as any policies and procedures of the organizations to which the professional belongs. Computing professionals must abide by these rules unless there is a compelling ethical justification to do otherwise. Rules that are judged unethical should be challenged. A rule may be unethical when it has an inadequate moral basis or causes recognizable harm. A computing professional should consider challenging the rule through existing channels before violating the rule. A computing professional who decides to violate a rule because it is unethical, or for any other reason, must consider potential consequences and accept responsibility for that action.

2.4 Accept and provide appropriate professional review.

High quality professional work in computing depends on professional review at all stages. Whenever appropriate, computing professionals should seek and utilize peer and stakeholder review. Computing professionals should also provide constructive, critical reviews of others' work.

2.5 Give comprehensive and thorough evaluations of computer systems and their impacts, including analysis of possible risks.

Computing professionals are in a position of trust, and therefore have a special responsibility to provide objective, credible evaluations and testimony to employers, employees, clients, users, and the public. Computing professionals should strive to be perceptive, thorough, and objective when evaluating, recommending, and presenting system descriptions and alternatives. Extraordinary care should be taken to identify and mitigate potential risks in machine learning systems. A system for which future risks cannot be reliably predicted requires frequent reassessment of risk as the system evolves in use, or it should not be deployed. Any issues that might result in major risk must be reported to appropriate parties.

2.6 Perform work only in areas of competence.

A computing professional is responsible for evaluating potential work assignments. This includes evaluating the work's feasibility and advisability, and making a judgment about whether the work assignment is within the professional's areas of competence. If at any time before or during the work assignment the professional identifies a lack of a necessary expertise, they must disclose this to the employer or client. The client or employer may decide to pursue the assignment with the professional after additional time to acquire the necessary competencies, to pursue the assignment with someone else who has the required expertise, or to forgo the assignment. A computing professional's ethical judgment should be the final guide in deciding whether to work on the assignment.

2.7 Foster public awareness and understanding of computing, related technologies, and their consequences.

As appropriate to the context and one's abilities, computing professionals should share technical knowledge with the public, foster awareness of computing, and encourage understanding of computing. These communications with the public should be clear, respectful, and welcoming. Important issues include the impacts of computer systems, their limitations, their vulnerabilities, and the opportunities that they present. Additionally, a computing professional should respectfully address inaccurate or misleading information related to computing.

2.8 Access computing and communication resources only when authorized or when compelled by the public good.

Individuals and organizations have the right to restrict access to their systems and data so long as the restrictions are consistent with other principles in the Code. Consequently, computing professionals should not access another's computer system, software, or data without a reasonable belief that such an action would be authorized or a compelling belief that it is consistent with the public good. A system being publicly accessible is not sufficient grounds on its own to imply authorization. Under exceptional circumstances a computing professional may use unauthorized access to disrupt or inhibit the functioning of malicious systems; extraordinary precautions must be taken in these instances to avoid harm to others.

2.9 Design and implement systems that are robustly and usably secure.

Breaches of computer security cause harm. Robust security should be a primary consideration when designing and implementing systems. Computing professionals should perform due diligence to ensure the system functions as intended, and take appropriate action to secure resources against accidental and intentional misuse, modification, and denial of service. As threats can arise and change after a system is deployed, computing professionals should integrate mitigation techniques and policies, such as monitoring, patching, and vulnerability reporting. Computing professionals should also take steps to ensure parties affected by data breaches are notified in a timely and clear manner, providing appropriate guidance and remediation.

To ensure the system achieves its intended purpose, security features should be designed to be as intuitive and easy to use as possible. Computing professionals should discourage security precautions that are too confusing, are situationally inappropriate, or otherwise inhibit legitimate use.

In cases where misuse or harm are predictable or unavoidable, the best option may be to not implement the system.

3. PROFESSIONAL LEADERSHIP PRINCIPLES.

Leadership may either be a formal designation or arise informally from influence over others. In this section, "leader" means any member of an organization or group who has influence, educational responsibilities, or managerial responsibilities. While these principles apply to all computing professionals, leaders bear a heightened responsibility to uphold and promote them, both within and through their organizations.

A computing professional, especially one acting as a leader, should...

3.1 Ensure that the public good is the central concern during all professional computing work.

People—including users, customers, colleagues, and others affected directly or indirectly—should always be the central concern in computing. The public good should always be an explicit consideration when evaluating tasks associated with research, requirements analysis, design, implementation, testing, validation, deployment, maintenance, retirement, and disposal. Computing professionals should keep this focus no matter which methodologies or techniques they use in their practice.

3.2 Articulate, encourage acceptance of, and evaluate fulfillment of social responsibilities by members of the organization or group.

Technical organizations and groups affect broader society, and their leaders should accept the associated responsibilities. Organizations—through procedures and attitudes oriented toward quality, transparency, and the welfare of society—reduce harm to the public and raise awareness of the influence of technology in our lives. Therefore, leaders should encourage full participation of computing professionals in meeting relevant social responsibilities and discourage tendencies to do otherwise.

3.3 Manage personnel and resources to enhance the quality of working life.

Leaders should ensure that they enhance, not degrade, the quality of working life. Leaders should consider the personal and professional development, accessibility requirements, physical safety, psychological well-being, and human dignity of all workers. Appropriate human-computer ergonomic standards should be used in the workplace.

3.4 Articulate, apply, and support policies and processes that reflect the principles of the Code.

Leaders should pursue clearly defined organizational policies that are consistent with the Code and effectively communicate them to relevant stakeholders. In addition, leaders should encourage and reward compliance with those policies, and take appropriate action when policies are violated. Designing or implementing processes that deliberately or negligently violate, or tend to enable the violation of, the Code's principles is ethically unacceptable.

3.5 Create opportunities for members of the organization or group to grow as professionals.

Educational opportunities are essential for all organization and group members. Leaders should ensure that opportunities are available to computing professionals to help them improve their knowledge and skills in professionalism, in the practice of ethics, and in their technical specialties. These opportunities should include experiences that familiarize computing professionals with the consequences and limitations of particular types of systems. Computing professionals should be fully aware of the dangers of oversimplified approaches, the improbability of anticipating every possible operating condition, the inevitability of software errors, the interactions of systems and their contexts, and other issues related to the complexity of their profession—and thus be confident in taking on responsibilities for the work that they do.

3.6 Use care when modifying or retiring systems.

Interface changes, the removal of features, and even software updates have an impact on the productivity of users and the quality of their work. Leaders should take care when changing or discontinuing support for system features on which people still depend. Leaders should thoroughly investigate viable alternatives to removing support for a legacy system. If these alternatives are unacceptably risky or impractical, the developer should assist stakeholders' graceful migration from the system to an alternative. Users should be notified of the risks of continued use of the unsupported system long before support ends. Computing professionals should assist system users in monitoring the operational viability of their computing systems, and help them understand that timely replacement of inappropriate or outdated features or entire systems may be needed.

3.7 Recognize and take special care of systems that become integrated into the infrastructure of society.

Even the simplest computer systems have the potential to impact all aspects of society when integrated with everyday activities such as commerce, travel, government, healthcare, and education. When organizations and groups develop systems that become an important part of the infrastructure of society, their leaders have an added responsibility to be good stewards of these systems. Part of that stewardship requires establishing policies for fair system access, including for those who may have been excluded. That stewardship also requires that computing professionals monitor the level of integration of their systems into the infrastructure of society. As the level of adoption changes, the ethical responsibilities of the organization or group are likely to change as well. Continual monitoring of how society is using a system will allow the organization or group to remain consistent with their ethical obligations outlined in the Code. When appropriate standards of care do not exist, computing professionals have a duty to ensure they are developed.

4. COMPLIANCE WITH THE CODE.

A computing professional should...

4.1 Uphold, promote, and respect the principles of the Code.

The future of computing depends on both technical and ethical excellence. Computing professionals should adhere to the principles of the Code and contribute to improving them. Computing professionals who recognize breaches of the Code should take actions to resolve the ethical issues they recognize, including, when reasonable, expressing their concern to the person or persons thought to be violating the Code.

4.2 Treat violations of the Code as inconsistent with membership in the ACM.

Each ACM member should encourage and support adherence by all computing professionals regardless of ACM membership. ACM members who recognize a breach of the Code should consider reporting the violation to the ACM, which may result in remedial action as specified in the ACM's Code of Ethics and Professional Conduct Enforcement Policy.

The Code and guidelines were developed by the ACM Code 2018 Task Force: Executive Committee Don Gotterbarn (Chair), Bo

Brinkman, Catherine Flick, Michael S Kirkpatrick, Keith Miller, Kate Varansky, and Marty J Wolf. Members: Eve Anderson, Ron Anderson, Amy Bruckman, Karla Carter, Michael Davis, Penny Duquenoy, Jeremy Epstein, Kai Kimppa, Lorraine Kisselburgh, Shrawan Kumar, Andrew McGettrick, Natasa Milic-Frayling, Denise Oram, Simon Rogerson, David Shamma, Janice Sipior, Eugene Spafford, and Les Waguespack. The Task Force was organized by the ACM Committee on Professional Ethics. Significant contributions to the Code were also made by the broader international ACM membership. This Code and its guidelines were adopted by the ACM Council on June 22nd, 2018.

This Code may be published without permission as long as it is not changed in any way and it carries the copyright notice. Copyright (c) 2018 by the Association for Computing Machinery.

Appendix 2 Full Source Code Listings

Listing 8. ImageTool

```
package us.daconta.lazy.programmers.examples;

import java.awt.BorderLayout;
import java.awt.Dimension;
import java.awt.Graphics;
import java.awt.Image;
import java.awt.Rectangle;
import java.awt.image.BufferedImage;
import java.io.File;
import java.io.IOException;
import javax.imageio.ImageIO;
import javax.swing.ImageIcon;
import javax.swing.JFrame;
import javax.swing.JLabel;
import javax.swing.JPanel;

/**
 *
 * @author mdaconta
 */
public class ImageTool extends JFrame
{
    private BufferedImage image;
    public ImageTool(String fullpath) throws IOException
    {
        this(new ImageIcon(fullpath));
    }

    public ImageTool(BufferedImage img)
    {
        this(new ImageIcon(img));
    }

    public ImageTool(ImageIcon icon)
    {
```

```java
        super("Image Frame");
        image = imageToBufferedImage(icon.getImage());
        JLabel imgLabel = new JLabel();
        imgLabel.setIcon(icon);
        JPanel panel = new JPanel();
        panel.add(imgLabel);
        setDefaultCloseOperation(javax.swing.WindowConstants.EXIT_ON_CLOSE);
        getContentPane().add(panel);
        pack();
    }

    public static BufferedImage imageToBufferedImage(Image img)
    {
        BufferedImage bufImg = new BufferedImage
        (img.getWidth(null),img.getHeight(null),BufferedImage.TYPE_INT_RGB);
        Graphics graphics = bufImg.getGraphics();
        graphics.drawImage(img, 0, 0, null);
        graphics.dispose();
        return bufImg;
    }

    public BufferedImage getImage()
    {
        return image;
    }

    public BufferedImage getSubImage(Rectangle r)
    {
        BufferedImage subImage = null;
        if (image != null)
        {
            Rectangle imgRect = new Rectangle(0, 0, image.getWidth(),
                                              image.getHeight());
            if (r != null && imgRect.contains(r))
            {
                subImage = image.getSubimage(r.x, r.y, r.width, r.height);
            }
        }
        return subImage;
    }

    public static void main(String [] args)
    {
```

```
    try
    {
        ImageTool imgFrame = new ImageTool(args[0]);
        imgFrame.setVisible(true);
        int x = Integer.parseInt(args[1]);
        int y = Integer.parseInt(args[2]);
        int width = Integer.parseInt(args[3]);
        int height = Integer.parseInt(args[4]);
        BufferedImage subImage = imgFrame.getSubImage(new
                                        Rectangle(x,y,width,height));
        ImageTool subImageFrame = new ImageTool(subImage);
        subImageFrame.setVisible(true);
    } catch (Throwable t)
      {
        t.printStackTrace();
      }
  }
}
```

Listing 9. ImageToolTest

```
package us.daconta.lazy.programmers.examples;

import java.awt.Image;
import java.awt.Rectangle;
import java.awt.image.BufferedImage;
import java.awt.image.Raster;
import java.io.IOException;
import org.junit.jupiter.api.Test;
import static org.junit.jupiter.api.Assertions.*;

/**
 * JUnit tests for ImageTool class.
 * @author mdaconta
 */
public class ImageToolTest {

    private boolean comparePixels(BufferedImage image1, BufferedImage image2) {
        int width = image1.getWidth();
        int height = image1.getHeight();
        int width2 = image2.getWidth();
        int height2 = image2.getHeight();
        if (width != width2 || height != height2) {
            return false;
```

```java
  }

  for (int row = 0; row < height; row++) {
    for (int col = 0; col < width; col++) {
      if (image1.getRGB(col,row) != image2.getRGB(col,row))
      {
        return false;
      }
    }
  }
  return true;
}
/**
 * Test of getSubImage method, of class ImageTool.
 */
@org.junit.jupiter.api.Test
public void testGetSubImage() throws IOException {
  System.out.println("Testing getSubImage");
  ImageTool instance = new ImageTool(
      "C:\\Users\\mdaconta\\Documents\\ paycheck-programmer.jpg");
  BufferedImage image = instance.getImage();
  System.out.println("Test #1: null");
  Rectangle r = null;
  BufferedImage expResult = null;
  BufferedImage result = instance.getSubImage(r);
  assertEquals(expResult, result);

  /* Note: these would all be separately viewed and validated against a known
     image for correctness or even better, generated programmatically in a
     standard, synthetic test pattern. */
  BufferedImage upperEdge = image.getSubimage(0, 0, image.getWidth(), 1);
  BufferedImage lowerEdge = image.getSubimage(0, image.getHeight() - 1,
                                              image.getWidth(),1);
  BufferedImage rightEdge = image.getSubimage(image.getWidth() - 1, 0, 1,
                                              image.getHeight());
  BufferedImage leftEdge = image.getSubimage(0, 0, 1, image.getHeight());
  BufferedImage upperLeftCorner = image.getSubimage(0, 0, 1, 1);
  BufferedImage upperRightCorner = image.getSubimage(image.getWidth() - 1,
                                              0, 1, 1);
  BufferedImage lowerLeftCorner = image.getSubimage(0, image.getHeight() -
                                              1, 1, 1);
  BufferedImage lowerRightCorner = image.getSubimage(image.getWidth() - 1,
                                              image.getHeight() - 1, 1, 1);
```

```
System.out.println("Test #2: zeroes");
r = new Rectangle(0,0,0,0);
expResult = null;
result = instance.getSubImage(r);
assertEquals(expResult, result);

System.out.println("Test #3: negative");
r = new Rectangle(-1,1,1,1);
expResult = null;
result = instance.getSubImage(r);
assertEquals(expResult, result);

// upper edge
System.out.println("Test #4: upper edge");
r = new Rectangle(0,0,image.getWidth(),1);
int expectedWidth = image.getWidth();
int expectedHeight = 1;
result = instance.getSubImage(r);
assertResults(result, upperEdge, expectedWidth, expectedHeight);

// lower edge
System.out.println("Test #5: lower edge");
r = new Rectangle(0, image.getHeight() - 1, image.getWidth(),1);
expectedWidth = image.getWidth();
expectedHeight = 1;
result = instance.getSubImage(r);
assertResults(result, lowerEdge, expectedWidth, expectedHeight);

// left egde
System.out.println("Test #6: left edge");
r = new Rectangle(0, 0, 1, image.getHeight());
expectedWidth = 1;
expectedHeight = image.getHeight();
result = instance.getSubImage(r);
assertResults(result, leftEdge, expectedWidth, expectedHeight);

// right edge
System.out.println("Test #7: right edge");
r = new Rectangle(image.getWidth() - 1, 0, 1, image.getHeight());
expectedWidth = 1;
expectedHeight = image.getHeight();
result = instance.getSubImage(r);
```

```
        assertResults(result, rightEdge, expectedWidth, expectedHeight);

        // UL corner
        System.out.println("Test #8: UL corner");
        r = new Rectangle(0, 0, 1, 1);
        expectedWidth = 1;
        expectedHeight = 1;
        result = instance.getSubImage(r);
        assertResults(result, upperLeftCorner, expectedWidth, expectedHeight);

        // UR corner
        System.out.println("Test #9: UR corner");
        r = new Rectangle(image.getWidth() - 1, 0, 1, 1);
        expectedWidth = 1;
        expectedHeight = 1;
        result = instance.getSubImage(r);
        assertResults(result, upperRightCorner, expectedWidth, expectedHeight);

        // LL corner
        System.out.println("Test #10: LL corner");
        r = new Rectangle(0, image.getHeight() - 1, 1, 1);
        expectedWidth = 1;
        expectedHeight = 1;
        result = instance.getSubImage(r);
        assertResults(result, lowerLeftCorner, expectedWidth, expectedHeight);

        // LR corner
        System.out.println("Test #11: LR corner");
        r = new Rectangle(image.getWidth() - 1, image.getHeight() - 1, 1, 1);
        expectedWidth = 1;
        expectedHeight = 1;
        result = instance.getSubImage(r);
        assertResults(result, lowerRightCorner, expectedWidth, expectedHeight);
    }

    private void assertResults(BufferedImage result, BufferedImage expectedResult,
                int expectedWidth, int expectedHeight)
    {
        assertNotNull(result);
        assertEquals(result.getWidth(), expectedWidth);
        assertEquals(result.getHeight(), expectedHeight);
        assertTrue(comparePixels(result, expectedResult));
    }
```

```
}
```

Index

D

E

F

G

www.ingramcontent.com/pod-product-compliance
Lightning Source LLC
LaVergne TN
LVHW051537050326
832903LV00033B/4306